Divinely Dressed

Putting on Garments of Grace

Divinely Dressed

Putting on Garments of Grace

PENNY J. KENDALL

 BATHUNO PRESS

"These words will touch and challenge you to consider your spiritual wardrobe, and what changes may need to be made to better reflect your true identity in Christ. As you are challenged, may these grace-filled truths inspire and encourage you. These lessons are from the heart of a woman *Divinely Dressed* herself. May you be blessed, as I have, to learn from her."

—*Courtney Steed*, Speaker, and Author of <u>Everything You Need</u>

"Penny invites you to enjoy going through your spiritual closet, to find the perfect outfit to wear as you walk toward heaven with your loving Savior. You will enjoy looking into God's mirror to see yourself reflecting His glory. You will feel beautiful because you know He is happy with what you have chosen to put on."

—*Judy Warpole*, Missionary Wife, Speaker, and Author of <u>The Pleasure of His Company</u>

"We worry so much about what we wear on the outside—our dress, shoes, lipstick, jewelry. But in *Divinely Dressed*, Penny Kendall reminds us of what REALLY matters—our spiritual wardrobe. Penny is a gifted teacher and writer. I highly recommend you read *Divinely Dressed* today. You will be encouraged and blessed."

—*Terilee Harrison*, International Speaker, Book Writing Coach and Author of <u>The Shameless Life</u>

"This book is truly inspirational. As a result of reading *Divinely Dressed*, a "spring cleaning" has taken place in my spiritual closet. Old garments have been replaced with Garments of Grace as I strive to live my life as a daughter of the King."

—*Don-Ann Wheeler*, Author of <u>Basic Bible Skills: Building Blocks for a Firm Foundation</u>

"I recently had opportunity to read Penny Kendall's book *Divinely Dressed: Putting on Garments of Grace*, and I saw the admonition to "wear" our faith in a different light than I ever had before.

The analogy of removing our sin-stained garments and putting on the attributes of Christ is beautifully illustrated in the modern concept of an extreme makeover, and Penny does a wonderful job of making that scene come to life. She takes us from our "used-to-be" state as sinners in need of redemption to our "meant-to-be" state as we grow in maturity and grace, adding the qualities and spiritual wisdom that comes with new life in Christ.

The book is a valuable combination of biblical commands and encouragement, coupled with Penny's true-to-life examples of how this happens in real time. How do we transition from people with our human flaws and weaknesses to spiritual beings full of grace and ability to forgive? How do we bring our speech and behavior in line with Christ-like love and values? Penny reminds us that our value and definition of self no longer comes from other people, or even from ourselves, but from the way God defines us: chosen, redeemed, saved, forgiven, accepted—all these terms and more are our new identity in Christ.

Each chapter has specific, down-to-earth examples of how to make these changes come to life, and each chapter has follow up questions perfect for personal reflection, or for interaction if you're using the book in a class setting. Some of the advice I found most helpful was Penny's specific and insightful knowledge of how to speak to those dealing with the loss of loved ones—how to be with those who mourn and hurt, when we feel so inadequate.

I know you'll appreciate Penny's gentle guidance and wisdom as she shares from her heart, and takes you from a place of "used-to-be" to "meant-to-be." It was the perfect encouragement for me, and I hope you'll include this book on your list of "must-reads" for the coming year!"

—*Sheila Gibson*, Author of <u>Choose Your Purpose, Love Your Life</u>

Dedication

To Casandra Martin, a seeker of the Word and a lovely example of what it looks like to wear garments of grace.

Thank you for beginning a legacy of relishing in God's word, and for allowing me to share in it with you.

You are loved—and greatly missed.

Contents

$\mathcal{A}$cknowledgements

To my *Father in Heaven*, who redeemed me and chose me as His own. Thank you for entrusting me with the message these pages contain. You are my ALL-IN-ALL.

To my husband, *Brandi*, who has shared life, walked on mission, and built legacy with me. Thank you for being my spiritual guide, my confidant, my greatest encourager, and my best friend. You are the man of my dreams.

To my *legacy*, my six amazing children (*Courtney, Amber, Lacey, Dustin, Jared, and Kayli*) and twelve grandchildren, who have filled my life with love, joy, laughter, and purpose. Thank you for teaching me what true riches are. You are my treasured ones.

To my son, *Dustin*, who took his first step into Paradise from Iraq in 2006. His leaving has taken me to the darkest places—and to the loveliest of places, I've ever been. Thank you for teaching me the depth of comfort and compassion. You are my beauty among ashes, my rose among thorns. You are my *Dusty Rose*. I miss you.

To my long-time friend, *Deb*, who has always been an example of what God's woman should look like; a sharer of wisdom and many of the "isms" I live by each day. Thank you for walking my Christ-life with me. You are dear to my heart.

To my *Jesus Circle*; my precious friends who have stuck with me, believed in me, and loved me with God-love. Thank you for encouraging me on my journey as I wrote the words in this little book. You are among my greatest blessings.

$\mathcal{S}$HE STOOD IN SHOCKED SILENCE as the style expert held up each piece of clothing from her closet, shook her head in disapproval, and deposited them one by one into a nearby trash bin. Her wardrobe was a disaster, not at all appropriate for the woman she wanted and was meant to be. That was about to change.

She was about to receive an extreme makeover. The hair stylists, make-up artists, and counselors clamored about her; all intent and on a mission to give her new eyes and to reveal the beauty she had hidden beneath her outer mess. Her old, tattered clothes were discarded and replaced with lovely garments more befitting her true identity. When she stepped from behind the curtain to her awaiting friends and family, her excitement shined brightly from her smiling eyes.

Divinely Dressed: Putting on Garments of Grace will be your *spiritual* makeover; your transformation journey to finding true identity in Christ, to seeing yourself through His eyes, and to exchanging the old clothes of the world for garments so full of grace that the image of His glory will radiate from your life onto those around you.

"... You have taken off your old self with its practices and have put on the new self, which is being renewed in knowledge in the image of its Creator" (Colossians 3:9,10 NIV).

Identification Review
Chapter 1

THE APOSTLE PAUL WAS IMPRISONED in Rome when Epaphras, his fellow minister in Christ, brought a report of the Colossian and Laodicean churches.

His letter back to the church in Colossae reflects his thanks to God for their faithfulness and love, his prayer that they live a life worthy of the Lord, and his concern that in spite of their dedication, they were being deceived by wise-sounding philosophies that had no truth. Their true identity in Christ was being hidden by their attempt to hang on to old practices while still serving Him. They were essentially trying to wear their Christ-clothes over their earthly ones, and who they were, was being covered.

They needed a reminder of their Christ identity, an identification review, to help them fully understand and grasp who they already were as children of the King.

CHRIST: THE IMAGE OF THE INVISIBLE GOD

At the time of Paul's writing to the Colossians, about 60 AD, there were many false religions and heresies that attacked the supremacy and authority of Christ, and tried to impose rules that were based on human commands and teachings. Paul's concern that Christ's followers were being deceived by the fine-sounding arguments of these false teachers was great. He told them, *"I want you to know how much I am struggling for you and for those at Laodicea"* (Colossians 2:1).

Though Paul likely had never met the brethren in Colossae, his love for them was obviously deep. His use of the Greek word *agon* (struggling) is where we get our English word, agony. This word was used to indicate "a contest of athletes, runners, charioteers; a grueling conflict.[1]" By using this specific word, Paul implied he was figuratively contending or fighting with Satan for the minds and hearts of the brethren in Colossae and Laodicea.

Paul says he was *agonizing* over what he'd heard was happening there, and he implored them to listen carefully. It was important that they understood the truth of who Christ was, in contrast to what they were being told.

This, he said, is who Christ is:

- *"He is the image of the invisible God, the firstborn over all creation"* (Colossians 1:15).

- *"He is before all things, and in him all things hold together"* (Colossians 1:17).

- *"And he is the head of the body, the church; he is the beginning and the firstborn from among the dead, so that in everything he might have the supremacy"* (Colossians 1:18).

- *"For in Christ all the fullness of the Deity lives in bodily form ... who is the head over every power and authority"* (Colossians 2:9-10).

The struggle for the hearts of Christ's followers is just as strong today as it was in 60 AD. We are inundated with distorted understanding and criticism of who our Lord is. His authority and supremacy is in constant question. False religions and worldly thinkers try to impose their human traditions and teachings *"that have an appearance of wisdom ... but they lack any value"* (Colossians 2:23, NIV), with their faulty notions that somehow we can embrace and practice these ideas while still serving Him.

"So then, just as you received Christ Jesus as Lord, continue to live your lives in Him, rooted and built up in him, strengthened in the faith as you were taught, and overflowing with thankfulness. See to it that no one takes you captive through hollow and deceptive philosophy, which depends on human tradition and the elemental spiritual forces of this world rather than on Christ" (Colossians 2:6-8).

Living a dual life is not possible for those who belong to Him. The ways of the world and the ways of Christ do not agree nor can they walk in unison with one another. They never can. He will not share His glory with other gods or idols in our lives. He cannot and will not be just one of our many masters. He must be the only one we serve—*the only One.*

WITHOUT HIM WE WOULD BE NOTHING

To say that I came to the foot of the cross with a lot of baggage full of dirty laundry would be an understatement. I didn't need just a sprinkling of grace; I needed it poured on me. The blood-bought redemption the Lord offered the mess that I was made no sense. Yet, He chose me. He reached down and gathered the pieces of my broken life and set my feet on a new, not-always-easy journey toward Him and my *meant-to-be.*

The apostle Paul knew this feeling all too well. Before his conversion to Christ, he was zealous in his persecution of Christians, often going to great lengths to pursue and murder them, feeling duty-bound and justified to do so. But, Jesus chose him, too. He reached down and plucked Paul out of his self-assured, self-focused life and set him on a new, not-so-easy path toward his God-planned purpose.

Paul would later call himself the chief of all sinners and profess that it was only by the grace of God (and indeed it was), that Jesus had been revealed to him so that he was able to fulfill that purpose.

"For you have heard of my previous way of life in Judaism, how intensely I persecuted the church of God and tried to destroy it. I was advancing in Judaism beyond many of my own age among my people and was extremely zealous for the traditions of my fathers. But when God, who set me apart from my mother's womb and called me by his grace, was pleased to reveal his Son in me so that I might preach him among the Gentiles ..." (Galatians 1:13-16).

Sometimes I take for granted the gift I've received, forgetting who I was before He embraced me, took me in, and called me to His purpose. It's in those moments of forgetfulness that I need to step back and reflect on the generous blessings He's offered me by His rich mercies and His all-powerful grace. Not so I can live in the past or beat myself up for the mistakes I've made, but so that I can re-align myself with who He is and who I am *in* Him.

It was with this in mind that Paul reminded the Colossian brethren what they'd been blessed with, so they, too, could re-align their hearts and their behavior with who they were in Christ.

As if to say "faithful ones, do you remember?", he wrote,

- *"He has rescued us from the dominion of darkness"* (Colossians 1:13, NIV).

- *"Once you were alienated from God and were enemies in your minds because of your evil behavior"* (Colossians 1:21, NIV).

- *"You were dead in your sins"* (Colossians 2:13, NIV).

Just as importantly, do *we* remember?

Do we remember that without Christ we were nothing? Without Christ, our sins weighed us down. Without Christ, we were condemned to die and without hope. Without Him we were separated from His promise, excluded and lost.

"Remember that at that time you were separate from Christ, excluded from citizenship in Israel and foreigners to the covenants of the promise, without hope and without God in the world" (Ephesians 2:12).

The beautiful truth for those of us who have given our lives to Christ and have chosen to serve Him, is that even though we *were* nothing, we've been rescued from our sad condition and have been made into something special *in Him*.

You, my sweet sister, have been made into something special in Him!

YOU ARE WHO HE SAYS YOU ARE

In a world culture that focuses so much value and energy on what others think about your past successes and failures, physical appearance, money, stuff, and career, it's easy to believe the measure of your worth is decided that way. Enamored with outward proof of our significance, our false view of where our identity comes from can often leave us feeling inadequate, worthless, broken, and defeated; the opposite of who He intends for us to be.

Our true identity is not made of these things. Our true identity lies with the One who made us, died for us, redeemed us, and walks with us as we journey toward our meant-to-be. Our identity and our significance lies not with who others say we are, but with who *He* says we are.

My son was recently the target of a scam artist. This man, claiming to be an official from the Internal Revenue Service, quickly manipulated him into a position of fear and panic. Knowing just enough truth about who my son was, this swindler initially convinced him that he was indeed all he claimed to be. Not only were his lies woven with perfect precision, but he used my son's desire to do the right thing, to frighten him into believing he couldn't turn to anyone for help in his situation, not even his wife. It wasn't until the impostor began making a few tiny mistakes, until the fabric of his deception began to get a little tear in it, that my son was sure he was being duped. He would later say how he felt like a hostage in this situation; fearing that if he didn't do exactly what he was told, horrible things would happen. A ruthless enemy was actively at work that day, but thankfully, the truth eventually exposed him.

The enemy is actively at work in our lives, too. His lies are also woven with perfect precision. He knows just enough about us and our insecurities to convince us of the validity of his claims.

Even in our desire to be God's women, the enemy can direct us away from the source of our help and manipulate us into accepting that what he says about us is accurate. Persuaded by his lies, fear and self-doubt can overtake our hearts and hold us hostage with distortions of our true identity. These beliefs can cause us to be less than He meant for us to be. It is only by *His* truth that Satan's deceit can be exposed.

Write these truths on your heart:

You are LOVED — John 3:16-18a

You are THE DISPLAY OF HIS SPLENDOR — Isaiah 60:21

You are HIS MASTERPIECE — Ephesians 2:10 (NLT)

You are CHOSEN — 1 Peter 2:9

You are BLOOD BOUGHT — 1 Peter 1:18,19

You are REDEEMED — Galatians 3:14

You are MADE ALIVE — Colossians 2:13b-14

You are SAVED — Hebrews 5:8-9

You are FORGIVEN — Matthew 26:28

You are A NEW CREATION — 2 Corinthians 5:17

You are HEALED — 1 Peter 2:24

You are ACCEPTED — Romans 15:7

You are ADOPTED — Ephesians 1:5,6

You are part of HIS FAMILY; HIS BODY — Ephesians 4:16

You are ETERNAL — John 10:28

You are INSEPARABLE — Romans 8:38,39

The truth is—you, dear one, are who He says you are.

HE ENEMY HAS BEEN LYING to God's people since the beginning of time, seeking to convince us that we are different or less than He created us to be. Adam and Eve fell victim to the lie that they could be equal to God; the Colossian brethren were deceived into thinking they could hold on to the practices of their old religions while still serving the Master; and we are so often left believing that we are not good enough to be loved by Him—or others.

The enemy may be cunning, but his lies have no power over us. Who we are is not determined by the world's view. Who we are is determined by God's view. Our true identity lies in who He is and who we are in Him. We are who He says we are. We are daughters of the King. We are His, made in the image of Christ and clothed for the purpose of reflecting His glory.

You are His—chosen and dearly loved.

Bask in the knowledge and understanding of your true identity, and get ready. Your spiritual makeover is about to begin.

REFLECTION

1. What was it about the Colossian church for which Paul expressed gratefulness? If he wrote a letter to you, for what part of your Christian walk would he be grateful?

2. In Colossians 1:9, Paul said he'd been praying for them. What was it he was asking God to do for them?

3. What are some wise-sounding and human philosophies that are prevalent in today's culture? Which of them do you struggle to let go of?

4. What was your life like before you put on Christ?

5. How has your commitment to Him changed the person you were?

6. In Colossians 1:15-20, what are some ways that Paul describes who Jesus is?

7. What are some of the incorrect measures of significance that our culture tries to place on us?

8. Which of these areas do you struggle to live up to?

9. Looking at the list of "You Are" statements, which of these are the most meaningful? Why?

Out With The Old
Chapter 2

THEY HAD HEARD THE GOOD NEWS of the gospel, believed it, and received it. They were the holy and faithful of Colossae, raised with Christ—new creations with a new purpose. But receiving the full riches of their inheritance and becoming who they were meant to be would require not only embracing their true identity in Christ but in setting their hearts and minds on things above, walking daily with Him, and letting His glory shine through them. The ugly clothes they were still wearing from their used-to-be lives had to be removed and thrown away.

As God's holy and faithful in this generation, receiving the full riches of our inheritance and becoming the reflection of His glory demand that we also cling to who we are in Christ and rid ourselves of anything that keeps others from seeing Him in us.

"Since, then, you have been raised with Christ, set your hearts on things above, where Christ is, seated at the right hand of God. Set your minds on things above, not on earthly things. For you died, and your life is now hidden with Christ in God. When Christ, who is your life, appears, then you also will appear with him in glory" (Colossians 3:1-4).

THE CALL TO CHRIST-LIFE

Paul wrote this letter to the Colossians, inspired by the Holy Spirit, with the knowledge that today as *we* read his words, the message would be as relevant to us in our contemporary culture, as it was to them in theirs.

His reminder of our identity in Christ and what it means to us as ones chosen and dearly loved, carries with it a call to live a life that reflects who we are.

"So all of us who have had that veil removed can see and reflect the glory of the Lord. And the Lord—who is the Spirit—makes us more and more like him as we are changed into his glorious image" (2 Corinthians 3:18 NLT).

We are called not only to belong to Christ but to be Christ's likeness, *full of grace*, to the world around us.

Because we have been raised with Christ and are now new creations in Him, we must think differently than we did in the life we used to live. Our commitment to the One who has given us a new life, precious and set apart, requires we set our hearts and minds on things above. Setting our hearts isn't just noticing the things of Christ, it is an intentional seeking of Him and His ways; a looking to the cross as the backdrop for all of our decisions and actions, no matter how logical or illogical they may seem to the culture of our day.

I once read another makeover story, one of a talented but homeless man who had long struggled with hardship and addiction. When he was discovered and offered a fresh start, he was not only hurting on the inside, he was filthy, unkempt, and worn on the outside. His physical transformation started with the taking off of his foul and tattered clothes and was followed by a hot bath, a haircut, and a new wardrobe of clean clothes.

I think we would agree how useless it would have been to have simply put on his new clothes over his old ones, yet we often try to do that with our Christ clothes. We believe Him, serve Him, and even proclaim Him, but stubbornly hang on to the old clothes, the old habits and behaviors that just don't belong on His favored ones. Peter said, *"But you are a chosen people, a royal priesthood, a holy nation, God's special possession"* (1 Peter 2:9).

Children of the King should not wear the dirty and tattered clothes of those without hope. The clothes awaiting us are royal garments of grace intended to radiate His glory. They are ours to wear. But first, the dirty ones must go, each one, into the nearest trash bin.

PUT TO DEATH

"Put to death, therefore, whatever belongs to your earthly nature: sexual immorality, impurity, lust, evil desires and greed, which is idolatry. Because of these, the wrath of God is coming. You used to walk in these ways, in the life you once lived" (Colossians 3:5-7).

Since you died with Christ and He is your life, Paul says you must also put to death the things that belong to your earthly nature: things that are immoral, impure, evil, and unholy.

The word that Paul uses for "put to death" is a strong action word, *nekros*[1], in the original Greek language, meaning "no further life, no further place, no further influence." It is a term used by physicians to describe a body part that has died and is putrefying. It is a life-threatening condition and must be removed to save the life of the patient.

Paul's use of this term, in reference to us, drives home the urgency of removing these unholy things from our lives. This is not for future consideration; it is for right now. It is life-threatening. These self-indulgent, fleshly desires putrefy our Christ-life and can have no place or influence in our walk with Him. For the sake of our life with Him, if they exist in us, they must be cut away without delay.

STRIPPING IT AWAY FOR GOOD

But now you must also rid yourselves of all such things as these: anger, rage, malice, slander, and filthy language from your lips. Do not lie to each other, since you have taken off your old self with its practices and have put on the new self, which is being renewed in knowledge in the image of its Creator" (Colossians 3:8-10).

Paul's call to our Christ-life continues as he further entreats us to rid ourselves of anything that gets in the way of being like Him and accurately reflecting Him to others.

In verses eight and nine, he once again uses strong action words that are meant to convey urgency and finality; the importance of fully casting off or stripping something away, with no possibility of retrieving it. In his study of Colossians, Bob Martin suggests these words are used when "a person is hurriedly and frantically stripping off a filthy, soiled garment that needs to be destroyed or burned, such as garments that have been contaminated by an infectious disease. This kind of garment must be burned so that no one else will become infected."[2]

THE DISEASE THAT DESTROYS

When the tiniest of germs invades our body, our defense system immediately goes into action to fight it off. If our immune system is weak and unable to do away with it, the germ quickly moves in and takes a foothold. Once secure in its little plot of cellular space, it begins to multiply and build forces for greater battles against the whole body, ones that can eventually lead to devastating disease and even death.

The initial feeling of anger is a tiny germ that invades the soul: insecurity, disappointment, unfulfilled desires, unmet expectations, injury, pride. Whatever the cause, living present in the Spirit and having our hearts set on things above is our only defense against the enemy that, left unchecked, moves in to take a foothold. It multiplies and builds forces there; boiling, seething, souring, until it becomes a sickness that takes over our whole heart and refuses to heal.

Paul's list of sinful garments—anger, rage, malice, slander, filthy language, lying—is an intentional look at the progression from germ to death; death of Christ-living, death of influence, death of relationship, death of the soul.

Anger - temper, agitation, or impulse that leads on to speak harshly or rashly.

Rage - anger built up until it boils, resulting in outbursts or uncontrolled behavior.

Malice - the vicious ill-will toward someone with a desire to injure or do harm.

Slander - speaking evil or unkind of someone with the specific purpose of doing harm.

Filthy Language - incontrollable tongue, intended to abuse and degrade someone, especially those who offend or oppose.

Lying - deliberate untruthfulness meant to convey the wrong impression of someone.

These things, defined in this context, make it clear how quickly anger can gain a foothold in our hearts with one ugly behavior building on the one before, devastating the lives of others, diseasing our own lives, and making our true identity as Christ followers impossible to recognize.

No wonder Paul insisted these dirty clothes had to be stripped off and thrown away for good!

WORDS: THE POWER TO LIFE OR DEATH

When Paul spoke of putting off filthy language in Colossians 3, he was specifically addressing the angry tongue that spews words intended to hurt and defame.

As I pen these words, yet another issue has become a wild fire on social media and the Internet; the angry mob of opinion-sharers speaking from the shadows, making Paul's admonishment more important today than ever.

Scripture is laden with references to the power of the tongue and the weight of responsibility carried with it. Every word spoken or written, has the power to do one of two things; to either breathe life and energy, or to tear down and destroy. Words have power. Words matter.

"Do not let any unwholesome talk come out of your mouths, but only what is helpful for building others up according to their needs, that it may benefit those who listen. And do not grieve the Holy Spirit of God ..." (Ephesians 4:29,30, NIV).

God's Word, even as it confronts, offers the breath of life, and He admonishes our words do the same. Unwholesome words, "rotten, diseased, and useless"[3] words, are not to come out of our mouths. Why? Because God intended our words to encourage and build up; to breathe life and energy to those who hear them. When they don't; when our words tear down and hurt, not only do they dim the reflection of Christ in our lives, but they also grieve the Holy Spirit of God.

Let that thought sink in for a moment.

It may be easy to justify criticisms or judgments of others in our own minds. It may also be easy to put aside the call to encourage, build up, and benefit the ones to whom we are speaking because of something they did wrong or didn't do right. We may be able to recite a long list of reasons why this person doesn't deserve kind words or why that person deserves unkind ones. We may be able to convince ourselves that it's okay to join the hateful bandwagon that is supposedly standing up for what's right. We may persuade ourselves that we have important information or opinions that need to be shared, regardless whether it's hurtful, inaccurate, makes a person look bad, or damages one's reputation.

No matter our reasoning or excuses, the truth remains. Even when confrontational words are needed (and they sometimes are), how we offer them makes all the difference. Words that do not breathe life; words that tear down and destroy, not only displease Him but they also deeply grieve Him.

Oh, Lord, may I speak life with my words. May our words always speak life!

"We continually ask God to fill you with the knowledge of his will through all the wisdom and understanding that the Spirit gives, so that you may live a life worthy of the Lord and please him in every way" (Colossians 1:9-10).

*I*F WE ARE TO LIVE A LIFE pleasing to the Lord, growing and becoming all we are meant to be, we can't keep wearing the ugliness of who we once were.

As children of the King, we are called to put away the earthly things that used to rule our hearts; to think differently than we used to think. We are called to a new way of living—Christ-living; transformed into His likeness, full of grace and to reflect the Lord's glory so that others can see Him, know Him, and believe Him.

If we are to wear the glory of the King, we must set our hearts on things above and rid ourselves of anything that obscures our true identity as Christ followers. His garments are ready for our adorning, but we can't put them on over tattered and dirty clothes soiled with impure and unholy conduct. We must strip them from our lives and throw them away so we may be fitted for His garments of grace.

REFLECTION

1. What does it mean to you, to be called to a Christ-life?

2. Paul admonishes in Colossians 3:1 to "set your hearts on things above." How will you need to change your thinking to do this?

3. To what old habits and behaviors do you stubbornly hang on? Which of these may be life-threatening?

4. What did Paul mean when he said to "put to death" what belongs to your earthly nature?

5. What is keeping you from putting away the things that are threatening to your Christ-life?

6. Write Colossians 3:8-10. Underline any of the behaviors on Paul's list that are present in your life. How can you begin to rid yourselves of these things?

7. Read Ephesians 4:29,30. What does Paul say that words are meant to do?

8. Words can breathe life or can bring death. Who does Paul say is grieved when our words are unwholesome or hurtful?

9. Have you said words to others that have torn down instead of built up? If so, how will you resolve to breathe life into others with your words?

Putting on Garments of Grace
Chapter 3

BEHIND THE DOORS of my mother's closet was the power to turn my little-girl world into a fantasy of kings and castles and royal life. Sometimes, I would sneak in when she wasn't home and cradle each of the lovely garments she had saved for the most precious of occasions. But it was her gown of lavender silk, donned with endless rows of ruffles, that always captured my fancy and called me to slip it on. On my short stature, its length would make a flowing train that trailed for what seemed like miles behind me. I swirled, I bowed, I giggled. Wearing it made me feel like nobility, like I *belonged* to a king— his daughter, his princess, his beloved.

For you and I today, there is no need for fantasy. We are daughters of the King. We are His beloved. We belong to Him.

CLOTHE YOURSELVES

"All of you who were baptized into Christ have clothed yourselves with Christ" (Galatians 3:27).

More than once in his messages to the churches of Asia Minor, Paul exhorts the brethren to clothe themselves in the character of Christ, the royal garments pulled straight from the closet of the King.

The entirety of Scripture, from beginning to end, speaks often of clothing and being clothed. Many times these refer to the wearing of godly garments: righteousness, salvation, splendor.

This idea of being clothed isn't a grab-and-go accessory, like a beaded purse, to be used whenever the occasion is right. It is *"a covering, an encompassing; being securely girded, and wrapped up tight"*[1] in the garments that we put on. So, when Paul tells us to clothe ourselves in the things of Christ, he intended for them to totally encompass who we are—to completely cover us with those qualities, not to just use them now and then.

The purpose of clothing is three-fold: to protect, to identify, to beautify. All these things are accomplished as we put on the character (or *graces*, as we will call them) of Christ. In being completely wrapped up in the graces of Christ, we are protected by His covering, it becomes evident who we belong to, and we become the beautiful image of the King we serve. What an awesome thought that someday I may so look like Him, that no one should ever doubt whose daughter I am. That is my deepest desire. I know it is yours, as well.

MULTI-COLORED GARMENTS OF GRACE

We have been called to transformation. Our spiritual makeover has begun with the challenge to throw away our old clothes; to rid our hearts and minds of anything that gets in the way of being His image-bearer. Now it's time to put on our *new* clothes.

As a photographer, I am enamored by the tiny details of God's creation and even more in awe of the endless shapes, sizes, and colors of His magnificent artwork. He didn't make just one variety of flower, or butterfly, or insect; He made thousands. Because of His love for us, He blesses us every day with a stunning color palette that feeds our God-given desire for beauty and variety. He didn't choose to make nature all the same, and He didn't choose to create *us* all the same, either. We are all to be clothed in garments of His grace, to wear clothes that identify us with the King's household, but, each piece will be as unique as we are—multi-shaped, multi-sized, and multi-colored.

As we move into the discussion of our new wardrobe, be reminded that you are who God made you and the colors and shapes of your garments will be dependent on the personality and gifts He has designed just for you and your *meant-to-be*. Your clothes don't have to look like or be like mine or anyone else's. They only have to look like the One to whom you belong, Christ, the King, *"the one and only Son, who came from the Father, full of grace and truth"* (John 1:14b).

SEEING THROUGH GOD'S EYES

"Therefore, as God's chosen people, holy and dearly loved, clothe yourselves with compassion, kindness, humility, gentleness and patience" (Colossians 3:12).

When I lift my camera and look through the viewfinder, my perception immediately changes. My point of vision becomes more intentional and focused on what I can see through the lens than my eye did while taking in the whole scene. To fully grasp the beauty of His creation, I am challenged to look more closely at what I'm seeing—to look through God's eyes rather than my own.

I believe that's what He challenges us to do with people, too. He calls us to humbly and intentionally look at others, not with our human eyes that have a tendency to take in whole scenes and miss the details, but to see with His eyes—the eyes of His heart. When in humility I understand who I am, who God is, and who other people are to Him, my perception of them changes. With a grace perspective, I can be more focused on their hearts and circumstances, and I can be more willing to invest myself in meeting their needs.

Henry Nouwen said, *"Compassion asks us to go where it hurts, to enter into the places of pain, to share in brokenness, fear, confusion, and anguish. Compassion challenges us to cry out with those in misery, to mourn with those who are lonely, to weep with those in tears."* And, that's just what Jesus did.

Jesus showed kindness, compassion, and understanding to those He encountered. Though He had not experienced the guilt of adultery or the pain of leprosy, when He saw the hurts of those who had, He gently and tenderly ministered to them; doing what was needed to heal their hurts. He saw them, not with human eyes, but with the loving eyes of the Father.

When Jesus wept over Lazarus's death (John 11:1-35), I believe He did so out of compassion for Lazarus's family, not because He was sad he was gone. To Jesus, Lazarus was not gone. He knew that Lazarus had already walked in Paradise, and He knew

He was about to raise him from the dead. Yet, He did not try to talk those who loved him out of their grief. He didn't tell them that time would heal their hurts. He didn't scold them for their lack of faith, exhort them to be strong, or remind them that Lazarus was in a better place. Because of His compassion and His kindness, because He could see through the eyes of God's heart, Scripture tells us He simply wept.

We also have endless opportunities to show compassion, kindness, and gentleness. Though every circumstance and every grief is unique to each individual, no one is immune to pain, and no one is without need for these graces to be offered. Offering them requires us to be intentional to focus closely on those around us. We must watch for opportunities to meet needs and to grasp every chance to show what Jesus looks like.

COMPASSION FOR THE GRIEVING

In our more than thirty-five years of ministry, my husband and I have had many opportunities to reach out to the hurting and grieving. We've been well trained to deal with those who have suffered loss of many kinds and even though we've always found it heartbreaking and difficult, we used to think we had a decent understanding of how to do so. That was, until the day our lives turned upside down and our own *grief journey*[2] began.

With the death of our 21-year-old soldier son, and in sharing a new bond with others who've lost children, we became extremely aware that much of what we had been taught was grossly inadequate and often wrong.

Many times, unrealistic pressure is put on Christians who have suffered loss. Though we, as the King's children, *do not grieve like the rest of mankind, who have no hope"* (1 Thessalonians 4:13), we still hurt—and that's okay. Our faith is not measured by our grief. It is simply a response to love and loss. There is *"a time to weep and a time to laugh, a time to mourn and a time to dance"* (Ecclesiastes 3:4). God never asked us to pretend that we do not hurt. He only asks that we turn to Him in our pain rather than seeking worldly solutions to numb it.

We, like many, studied the popular "five stages of loss"[3] and like many, we believed that grief was a linear process of stages that when completed, would mean the end of grieving.

Unfortunately, not.

Grief is not linear. Grief is recurrent.

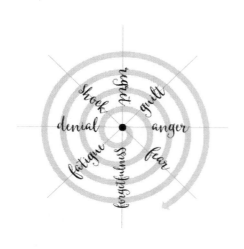

It is in my mind, more like a spiral with many grief responses, not stages, crossing through it. At the onset of our grief, we are at the middle of the spiral, and we visit all the responses at once: shock, denial, fear, anger, guilt, regret, and so on. As we continue on our grief journey (outwardly around the spiral), we visit these responses less often and less intensely, but we still visit them—over and over again.

These responses to grief not only apply to the death of a loved one but to other losses, as well: infidelity, divorce, infertility, miscarriage, prolonged illness, financial disaster, loss of friendship, loss of a home, death of a dream or vision.

When someone we care about is suffering, it is a natural response to try to do something or say something to make their pain go away. We don't want them to hurt. We want to make it stop for them. Unfortunately, this desire can often cause well-meaning people to share platitudes that can be far from encouraging or helpful.

What then can we do to offer comfort to those who are hurting?

Here are a few helpful tips:

- Be quietly present.
- Say "I'm sorry" and "I love you."
- Offer hugs.
- Weep with the weeping.
- Remember with them.
- Offer small expressions of love and service.
- Remember special days and "firsts."
- Allow them room to grieve, but don't forget them.
- Don't try to talk them out of their grief.
- Don't avoid the subject of their grief.
- Don't give unsolicited advice or try to explain why you think it happened.
- Don't expect them to be who they once were.
- Don't put a time limit on their grief.

Most of all, *be patient*.

Paul ties up the list of graces to be shown to others with the word *makrothumia*—patience. This word speaks of hanging in there, not giving up on people, and describes *"those engaged in the battle of life as compared to swimmers in the sea who seek safety on the shore[4]."*

The grieving process, no matter what the cause, is indeed a battle of life—a struggle for survival. Wearing the garments of kind and tender compassion often means being willing to swim patiently alongside someone, encouraging them not to give up, helping them when they get tired, and keeping them from sinking—for as long as it takes them to feel the safety of the shore.

WE HAVE BEEN RISEN WITH CHRIST. We are daughters of the King.

Our old and tattered clothes have been stripped away and lay heaped in a dirty pile on the floor. We stand fresh and clean before the royal closet, where new garments of grace hang majestically in preparation for our wearing. The grace clothes that await are no ordinary ones. Each one has been cut from the King's own linens and is uniquely fashioned for what He has made each of us to be.

There will be no question of our true identity. When wrapped up in the graces of Christ, it will become evident to Whom we belong. When Jesus saw the crowds, He saw not through human eyes, but through the eyes of the Father. His eyes were not fixed on outward appearances but on hearts, hurts, joys, and sorrows. He invested what was needed to minister to their deepest needs and to draw them close to the Father.

In wearing His garments of compassion, kindness, humility, gentleness, and patience, we will become the image of the King we serve. How we act, how we think, how we see, and how we care for others will be a reflection of His glory in us.

REFLECTION

1. "All who were baptized into Christ have _____
_____ __ _____." — Galatians 3:27

2. What does it mean to be "clothed in Christ"?

3. The three purposes of clothing are:

    a.

    b.

    c.

4. In Colossians 3:12, with what five graces does Paul tell us to clothe ourselves?

    a.

    b.

    c.

    d.

    e.

5. Read John 11:1-35. What did Jesus do to show compassion to the family of Lazarus when he died?

6. Name a few types of grief that someone may suffer.

7. What unrealistic pressure do you think may be placed on grieving Christians?

8. What are five common responses that may be attributed to the grief journey?

     a.

     b.

     c.

     d.

     e.

9. Referring to the helpful tips, what are some practical ways you can minister to a grieving friend or family member?

The Prisoner's Key

Chapter 4

OUR WOUNDED HEARTS sometimes struggle to understand and overcome the pain that is caused when we are deeply hurt by another. Feelings of injustice, betrayal, or rejection that go unacknowledged or unresolved, may make it difficult to let go and move forward. If not wrapped in the grace of Christ, these injuries can easily take root in unforgiveness.

"To forgive is to set a prisoner free and discover that the prisoner was you." —Lewis B. Smedes, *Forgive and Forget: Healing the Hurts We Don't Deserve*

Unforgiveness is a self-made prison that captures our heart and fills it with bitterness, resentment, anger, and distrust. It robs our joy and wraps heavy chains around our ability to see the beauty of God's blessings or lift our hearts in praise to Him. It sickens our souls and our relationships, dirties our garments of grace, and makes it impossible for His glory to be seen in us.

MY JOURNAL READS, "Oh, Lord, I feel so beaten and bruised. I am attacked from every side and I don't understand it. I've given up family and home and possessions to serve You here. My heart, though imperfect, has been pure. Now it hurts in ways I can't put into words. I beg you, Father, come to my defense. Show those who accuse me and have abused me, how wrong they are. Please, Lord, vindicate me and restore what I've lost."

A long-time friend had harshly accused me of something I wasn't guilty of doing, another dear friend had cut off ties because of a difficult situation I had nothing to do with, and a trusted fellow-worker in the kingdom had unexpectedly and hurtfully slandered my husband and me. It had all come in like a tornado sweeping through the camp, and the destruction had left me dazed. I didn't feel like I deserved the wounds that were being inflicted, and I struggled to let go of the frustrated emotions that were overwhelming me. My heart was broken at the injustice; my feelings were raw—and admittedly, so were some of my reactions. I felt defensive, and I wanted God to take up my cause.

What God would give me in each of these situations was not what I asked. Though God has often advocated for me in the midst of unfair treatment, it didn't appear He was doing so then. I wanted justice. I didn't get it. I wanted them to be sorry for how deeply they had injured me. If they were, I never knew it. I wanted Him to fix it all. He didn't. No matter how I prayed, no matter what I did, no matter how I fought to save what was so important to me, the thing I desperately desired never came to pass. Though He has proven often in my life that He does indeed fight for me, that would not be what He would make evident in this painful season.

What He would establish in me instead, was the key to unlocking the prison that threatened to hold me captive—a deeper understanding of what true forgiveness looks like.

THE GRACE OF PARDON

True forgiveness is a choice—not a choice to forget, but in the remembering, to respond differently than a person deserves. To bear no malice, to grant favor in kindness, to offer the grace of pardon[1].

It can be one of the most difficult yet one of the most beautiful graces God asks us to show to others. Implementing it can often feel more painful than the original wound itself. Yet, when making the choice to emotionally release the person who has injured our heart, we are also making the choice of freedom for ourselves.

JUST AS HE FORGAVE

"Bear with each other and forgive whatever grievances you may have against one another. Forgive as the Lord forgave you" (Colossians 3:13).

Though the words patience and forbearance are often used interchangeably in English, the Greek word *anechomai*[2] or forbearance, holds with it an even deeper meaning than the other. Forbearance requires the patience to stay the course with someone, but it is also enduring, tolerant, and restrained. It holds with it the meaning of putting off punishment for as long as possible; the way God put off punishing Israel for their continued disobedience (Isaiah 1:2ff). Because of Christ, God has also been tolerant of our shortcomings, has delayed our punishment, and instead, has offered us pardon from the cost of our sinful lives (Romans 3:23-26).

When I reflect on the life I used to live and the Christ-life I endeavor to live now, with all its imperfections and weaknesses, I am humbled by His compassion and kindness. I don't deserve the grace He pours on me, nor have I earned the blessings He bestows. For all the times I've felt unjustly accused, there are endless more in which I have been unjustly forgiven. Understanding the depth of my own sin, experiencing His saving grace every day, and realizing my condition without it, stretches me past my own perspective. Each time God asks me to forgive, even when it doesn't seem fair or just, I am reminded of the sacrifices that have been made on my behalf and my heart begins to soften to those who've hurt me. I think that must be how He planned it.

It seems significant that Paul would begin his clothing list in Colossians 3:12, with the heart-actions of compassion, kindness, gentleness, humility, and patience before he mentioned putting on the garment of forgiveness. Forgiveness isn't just for when it seems comfortable, as one would wear a coat or sweater when desired. It's to be worn all the time; a covering of the heart. It works in tandem with these other graces. Without them, our attempts at forgiveness would be feeble and superficial, at best.

This call to be clothed in forgiveness is about grasping the depth of our blessing and responding to it. It is not so that we will be forgiven but because we are forgiven. It comes not only as a condition of our own forgiveness, but also as a promise that because He has gifted it to us, we are more than able to gift it to others. Jesus never asks us to do anything He didn't do. Even though it may not be easy, we know that because Jesus did it, we can do it, too.

WHAT FORGIVENESS ISN'T

In the face of deep hurt, forgiveness can feel daunting and impossible. As Christians, we know we should do it; walking the grace-life calls for it. Even so, our hearts may struggle to hold on tightly to our wounds, fearing that if we let go, we will lose the only control we have left in our painful situation.

Fear and misconception can be our greatest barriers to letting go and claiming freedom through forgiveness. Understanding what forgiveness is, and what it is not, can give us victory over the battle within, and victory over the struggle to hold onto bitterness; to desire to take vengeance on the offender; to wish something bad for them; or to ration out our own form of justice.

C.S. Lewis wrote in Mere Christianity, "For a good many people imagine that forgiving your enemies means making out that they are really not such bad fellows after all, when it is quite plain that they are."

Forgiveness isn't accepting or condoning the wrongs of others. In the years of our ministry (and admittedly, in my own life), I've often seen a common road block to forgiving. When confronted with heartache, one of the most significant areas of resistance is the concern that forgiving someone would mean accepting or condoning their actions; saying that what the person did was okay or that it wasn't awful. The truth is, people do bad things for bad reasons. There are also good, godly people who do things that are hurtful and wrong. Offering the grace of forgiveness isn't the same as declaring another's innocence.

Forgiveness isn't pretending away or ignoring the actions of another. We live in an age of no accountability, even in the Lord's body. This might mean that the offender presumes the injured one should quietly sweep their offense under the rug, with no expectation of acknowledgment, sorrow, or apology. They might believe you should let them get away with whatever they've done in order to protect their reputation—possibly equating this expectation to grace. But that's not what forgiveness is. That's not what grace is.

John Ortberg says, "Grace always and only consists of what will help someone come home to the Father[3]". Christ, *"full of grace and truth"* (John 1:14), frequently confronted those who didn't walk according to His purpose. His goal was simple—to bring them home to the Father. This should be our goal, too. The grace of forgiveness doesn't have to pretend it never happened. It doesn't have to ignore the pain that has been inflicted. Being clothed in the grace of forgiveness might include disregarding the offense, but it may also need to include confronting with truth.

Forgiveness isn't dependent on the response of the other person. It can feel so unfair to be expected to forgive when the person who hurt you isn't sorry, they refuse to apologize, or try to blame you for their actions. If only they would care that they caused hurt and show remorse for what they'd done, it would be so much easier to let it go. If only they would do what they should do, it would be so much easier to do what I should do. Nevertheless, being clothed in forgiveness has nothing to do with them or how they respond to their offense. It has nothing to do with whether they ask for it or feel any remorse. It doesn't even have to do with whether the injured relationship is restored or not. Restoration and reconciliation take mutual commitment to that relationship. An intentional desire for mending coupled with honor, repentance, forgiveness, care, and trust is required by both parties. My choice to forgive, however, has everything to do with the condition of my own heart, and how I respond. My heart clothed in forgiveness, most importantly, protects my relationship with the Father.

Forgiveness isn't permission for further hurt. As I've counseled and comforted Christian women over the years, I've noticed another misconception about forgiveness. Committed to being all that God wants them to be, yet entrenched in abusive, immoral, or unfaithful marriages, they often struggle to understand what He would expect of them. These faithful women often feel pressured to defend, protect, and take responsibility for the actions of the other, allowing themselves to be convinced or bullied into believing that a godly woman's obligation is to stand by and subject herself to whatever is handed out. Faithful ones, hear my heart. The call to be clothed in forgiveness was never intended to be consent for continued abuse and mistreatment. The Father's love is far too great for that.

Forgiveness isn't taking responsibility for the actions of others. Paul's call to the Colossian church, and to us, is to be clothed in Christ, to wrap ourselves in tender mercies and forgiveness, and to bear with one another as we journey on. His exhortation to the Galatian brethren bears the same message. He urges them to carry one another's burdens (sins/weaknesses). Yet, he quickly reminds them that they *"should test their own actions and carry their own load"* (Galatians 6:2-5). In other words, they were responsible for their own behavior and had to accept the results that came with it. Although godly forgiveness does offer unwarranted compassion, it does not remove responsibility. Though it often offers undeserved emotional pardon, it does not remove the consequences of one's actions.

EHIND THE METAL BARS sits a young woman whose life has been replete with injustice, rejection, and abuse; her heart and body broken more times than she can recount. She had no control of it; it was all so unfair. Over the years, in an attempt at self-preservation, she has built a barrier of bitterness around the wounds of her soul and stays hidden inside the walls she has erected. Her heart is held captive by the injuries of her past and by the anger she has chosen to nurture and feed. The enemy has turned her fortress of protection into a prison that prevents her from living the abundant Christ-life God wants for her.

There is only one key that will unlock the heavy prison doors that hold the heart of this precious daughter of the King; only one key will unlock the prison that may be holding you captive, too—forgiveness.

Forgiveness is a supernatural grace. It does not come inherently. Extending it when deep wounds have been inflicted isn't easy. It can seem impossible. The enemy is ready to help you construct your fortress; to take your heart captive with bitterness and anger. Yet, for those whose heart is clothed in Christ, the enemy has no power to hold us.

You are a daughter of the King. You have the *key*.

REFLECTION

1. In what ways can unforgiveness build a prison around our hearts?

2. If you are struggling to let go of a hurt someone has inflicted on you, describe the wounds you feel.

3. Which of these areas of bondage has captured your heart in this situation?

4. *"When making the choice to emotionally release the person who has injured our heart, we are also making the choice of _____ for ourselves."*

5. Define *true forgiveness.*

6. How can understanding your own sin and redemption help you offer forgiveness to others?

7. What are five fears and misconceptions that may create barriers to offering forgiveness to others?

    a.

    b.

    c.

    d.

    e.

8. What is the greatest fear or misconception that keeps you from forgiving those who've hurt you?

9. What would be different if you chose to forgive the hurts you've been holding onto? What will you do to claim freedom from your bondage?

The Crimson Thread
Chapter 5

I WAS IN EIGHTH GRADE when I took my first home economics class. Sitting alongside us, as we beginners sewed straight skirts and drawstring bags, my teacher would fashion tailored dress shirts and double-breasted suits for her husband. The artistic desire she instilled in me then later bloomed into my own love of fabric and its creations: clothing, dolls, purses, household pretties, and quilts. Lots of quilts.

Though all of these are different than the other, there is one common element that must exist to make each creation complete—the thread. No matter how simple or elaborate the artistry, the thread is what fastens each together into what it is meant to be.

With Paul's challenge to put on the garments of grace comes the most essential element of love, which like thread, "... *binds them all together in perfect unity*" (Colossians 3:14).

"Let us love one another, for love comes from God. Everyone who loves has been born of God and knows God. Whoever does not love does not know God, because God is love. This is how God showed his love among us: He sent his one and only Son into the world that we might live through him ... but if we love one another, God lives in us and his love is made complete in us ... whoever lives in love lives in God, and God in him" (1 John 4:7-16).

AUTHENTICITY

Let's say you are interested in buying one of those multi-thousand-dollar, name-brand purses that you can only purchase in a ritzy store. I don't know anyone who has, mind you, and as for me, I can't imagine I'll ever be closer than a photograph to one. If, however, you were to do that, you'd want to have a guarantee that what you were spending your money on was the real thing. You'd need to check for all the unique elements that are supposed to be there to make sure you weren't getting a cheap imitation. You'd need to be sure it had that special embossed authenticity label that's only put in the genuine article.

In the ancient days of the kings, messages and edicts were authenticated in a similar way. Each scroll was sealed with wax and embossed with the king's signet ring. This was to insure it had come from him, not from someone claiming to be him.

We have been raised with Christ. We are children of the King. We have been called to clothe ourselves with the royal garments of grace. These garments can't be bought off the shelf of the nearest discount store. Each glorious outfit is unique and custom-made; cut from the King's finest linens, fashioned with the thread of His love running through it and holding it all together.

The love we have for one another is our mark of authenticity; the way *"everyone will know"* (John 13:34-35) that we're the genuine article. There are too often people who say they belong to Him but don't act like it. There are some who speak messages that claim to be from Him but grossly misrepresent who He is. Genuine love looks different than the world's love. When genuine love runs through everything we say and do, people will know that we belong to the King, that our message is from Him and no one else.

LOVE IS GOD

Throughout Scripture we can see four different attributes that are translated into the English word *love*. This love, the love that Paul says to *"put on"* in Colossians 3, is *agape*[1] love—God-Love. This unconditional and sacrificial love is not just a characteristic of

God or what He shows toward us. According to the apostle John, this love is what He is.

God is love.

Love is who God was before the foundation of the earth, before we were created. Love is who God has been through the ages and who He is now. Love is who God will always be: unfailing (Psalm 36:7), and forever enduring (Psalm 136).

Genuine love—is God.

It is this thread of God-love that is to be woven through our grace garments. It is this unique element that sets us apart and identifies who we are. It is not to be worn out of duty or obligation but as evidence of our real and intimate relationship with the King.

LOVE IS SELFLESS

"But God demonstrates his own love for us in this: While we were still sinners, Christ died for us" (Romans 5:8).

In an ultimate expression of love, Christ surrendered what was good for Him and took intentional action for our best. His demonstration of love wasn't just sacrificial; it was selfless. Sacrifice can be offered out of duty, but being selfless comes from a heart of love. He did what love demanded. There was only one way to bring us freedom and that required shedding His own blood unto death. He poured out everything needed to relieve the burdens of those He came to save. It was a crimson-colored love; a costly gift but offered freely.

God-love is always active (1 John 3:18); an intentional decision to meet the needs of others, even when it isn't easy or convenient to do so. Paul tells us in 2 Corinthians 8:2-3 that, *"In the midst of a very severe trial, their overflowing joy and their extreme poverty welled up in rich generosity ... they gave as much as they were able, and even beyond their ability."* The brethren acted on the needs they saw. They freely poured out all they had, even though it came at a great cost to them; they did it not out of obligation, but out of love.

Meeting the needs of others sometimes means meeting their physical needs. Sometimes, it means more. Sometimes it means we give our time, our heart, our emotions, and our honor.

LOVE HONORS

If it's true that God's heart is revealed by the amount of instruction He offers in certain areas, then there is no doubt that His heart is especially grieved by the sins of immorality, idolatry, and pride. It would also then be obvious that His heart is especially gladdened by those who demonstrate love through compassion, kindness, humility, and honor.

The idea that we are precious and honored in God's sight (Isaiah 43:4) is an awesome one, but throughout Scripture, we are also told that blessings await those who show honor—to Him and to others. We are promised that when we honor our father and mother, we will have a long life (Exodus 20:12). When we seek His way and His righteousness, we are promised deliverance, life, prosperity, and honor in return.

Showing honor can offer challenges, but the concept is a simple one. No matter how deeply we delve into it, the meaning is still clear: We are to respect, hold in high esteem, and value[2] the hearts and lives of others. By so doing, we honor our Father in heaven and our blessings overflow: *"Show proper respect to everyone, love the family of believers, fear God, honor the emperor"* (1 Peter 2:17).

Many cultures go to great lengths to guard against public humiliation or embarrassment, to cover up, sweep under the rug, or avoid addressing any issue that may cause someone to see them in a lesser light. Although this may sound admirable, it is not enough. These outward practices, like offering sacrifice, can be superficial. Honor is not superficial. It doesn't just put on a show.

True honor comes from a heart of love that humbly *"considers others better than ourselves"* (Romans 12:10). True honor requires that we exchange our view with His view, treasure others as He does, and authenticate our identity as children of the King.

LOVE SERVES

"Now that I, your Lord and Teacher, have washed your feet, you also should wash one another's feet. I have set you an example that you should do as I have done for you" (John 13:14-15).

Jesus said He had come to serve, not to be served. Then He did just that. He served.

They had been walking in sandals on the dusty Palestinian roads. Their feet were dirty from their travels and as was customary, they had to wash them before gathering around the table in the upper room to eat together. I bet they were a bit shocked when Jesus rose, took off His outer clothing, wrapped a towel around His waist, and began to wash their feet. This was not normally the duty of a king, but it was the mark of the true King. His life on earth was a constant example of what it means to humbly minister to the needs of those around Him and to put His love into action.

When we opened the door of our Estonian apartment that night, we saw two soldiers in dress uniforms standing before us. As if in slow motion, my eyes took in the scene: a soldier standing at attention, another addressing us by name, and over their shoulders, the faces of our dearest friends. The gray pallor of their expressions told me what I was about to hear would be devastating. It was. After the reading of the rote words and the formalities, we were left with our friends to absorb the news that our son had given his life that day on the battlefield of Iraq.

There is no way to share all that our friends did to minister to us that night—I'd need a whole chapter. But as I began to make those difficult phone calls to our family around the world, Deb stood quietly with her right hand on my shoulder. Never moving. Never wavering. Never complaining. It may seem like a meager thing, but it was no small gift to me. Those are moments I'll never forget. Even after all these years, I am still comforted with the knowledge that she was the image of God's love for me that night. Her ministry of presence was His reassurance of the promise that He would not leave me in my darkest hour. *"Where can I go from your Spirit? Where can I flee from your presence? ... Your right hand will hold me fast"* (Psalm 139: 7,10).

God-love is an intentional action. It doesn't just sit there. It gets up and serves. It doesn't have to be a big thing. You never know when a small thing will make a big difference. Bob Goff says that "love is never stationary ... it doesn't just keep thinking about it or keep planning for it. Simply put: love does.[3]" Indeed. God-love does!

"Now that you know these things, you will be blessed if you do them" (John 13:17).

LOVE STAYS

"Jesus knew that the hour had come for him to leave this world and go to the Father. Having loved his own who were in the world, he loved them to the end" (John 13:1).

I come from a long line of runners. When my world feels unsteady, my instinct is to do just that: to run, to pull away, to embrace my fear and hide. When it gets hard, my knee-jerk reaction is to call it off.

But Jesus didn't do that.

He knew what was about to happen. He knew what He was about to endure. It would be hard. It would be excruciating. He could have called it off. He could have run away—but He didn't. He loved them to the end. He stayed.

Working through the difficulties of a struggling or failing marriage can be rough. Standing by a child who's fallen into drugs or immorality can be painful. Seeing a friend fight cancer can be excruciating. Working through issues with our friends, our extended family, or our church family can take every bit of energy we have. Stopping to feed a homeless man or taking a meal to a widow can be inconvenient. It's normal to want to avoid pain or trouble. It's natural to want to run away.

God-love isn't natural. God-love isn't easy. God-love is selfless. God-love is intentional.

Our garments of grace do little, if not present. God-love stays to show compassion to the hurting, to offer kindness to the unkind, to be patient when it's hard, to serve when it's inconvenient—to extend forgiveness when it's undeserved. God-love stays to be the image of the risen King.

Worldly love runs away, but God-love stays to the end.

$\mathscr{G}$ OD'S HOLY PEOPLE were among those in Colossae; faithful brothers and sisters in Christ. They lived in a confusing time of varying religious beliefs and philosophies with practices that seemed to make sense to human thinking but were, in truth, counter to their true identity in Christ. Being pulled in every direction and often deceived by worldly ideas, it was sometimes difficult to discern who walked with Christ and who didn't.

We live in a confusing time, as well. We are surrounded by beliefs and philosophies that seem to make sense to our human reasoning but are in conflict with the wisdom of God. Even as Christ followers, we can fall prey to worldly viewpoints and find ourselves behaving in a way that makes it unclear that we are who we say we are.

Paul has challenged us, not only to clothe ourselves in the grace garments of Christ, but to bind each one together with crimson-colored thread: God-love that was expressed by His blood shed on a cross. This love will bring perfect unity. By this love *"everyone will know that you are my disciples"* (John 13:35).

When we wrap ourselves in the royal wardrobe and bind it all together with the thread of His love, there will be no mistaking; people will know we belong to the King.

REFLECTION

1. According to Paul in Colossians 3:14, what is the thread that binds us together in perfect unity?

2. We are children of the King. How will everyone know we are who we say we are?

3. What kind of love does Paul tell us to *put on*?

4. Describe *agape* love.

5. Name the four characteristics of God-love mentioned in this chapter.

    a.

    b.

    c.

    d.

6. What does it mean to show honor? What does God promise for those who do?

7. Read 2 Corinthians 8:2-3. What did the brethren do out of love for one another? How can you show love to the brethren in your church?

8. Read John 13:14-15. How did Jesus serve the disciples in the Upper Room?

9. Ponder five ways you can show God-love by serving in your family, church, or community. Write them here.

10. Even knowing what lay ahead, Jesus stayed — for our sake. From what hard things are you tempted to run away? For the sake of God-love, which ones will you purpose to stay with anyway?

Binding the Broken
Chapter 6

PEACE, QUIET, AND TRANQUILITY. That's what she used to say. Whenever I would ask my mom what she wanted for her birthday or Mother's Day or any other occasion, her answer was always the same: *"peace, quiet, and tranquility."*

I sometimes wished for those things in my mothering years, too. I would have loved a day of calm with the daily chores done by 10:00 a.m., everything in its place, and all six children holding hands and happily frolicking through the tall, swaying grasses. Can you hear me laughing right now?

What we sometimes envision and search for as peace is a world without chaos: no hurts, no troubles, no tensions. Ducks in a row. Perfect life.

No wonder it so often eludes us.

The peace of Scripture isn't this peace. Scriptural peace has little to do with what's going on around us and everything to do with what's going on within us.

BINDING THE BROKEN

Peace. We so desperately want it for our world and for ourselves. As a culture, we spend millions of dollars in pursuit of it, looking every direction to find what we believe will give us the peace we so desire. We struggle to fill the empty places that exist in our hearts, yet we so often fail to find what we seek. Is it possible we are looking for the wrong things in the wrong places?

Scripture is brimming with references of the peace promise. In Colossians 3:15, after challenging the church to be clothed in the King's wardrobe and to bind the garments together in love, Paul reminds them (and us) to *"let the peace of Christ rule in your hearts."*

His reference to peace in this context (the word *eirene*[1] in Greek) holds an awesome meaning. The word he uses in this encouragement means to *put it back the way it was supposed to be, to join together, to tie together in a whole, to make complete*—to bind or to mend what is broken.

Our world is broken. Turmoil surrounds us. Grief is poured out across the nations. A portion of the poem, *What They Did Yesterday Afternoon*[2] by Warsan Shire, aptly expresses that reality.

later that night
i held an atlas in my lap
ran my fingers across the whole world
and whispered
where does it hurt?
it answered
everywhere
everywhere
everywhere.

We, as Christians, are not immune to the tragedies and heartbreak that surround us. Difficulties in life are not respecters of persons. We are broken, and we hurt everywhere. How can there be peace in the midst of this?

In our pain, God gives us a longing to mend what is broken; a hunger to be complete and whole again. This longing is put there on purpose. It comes from the One who made us, to draw us to Him and to create a desire to find healing in Him. God has always wanted this for His people. His desire has always been for mended hearts and restored relationships.

True peace can't be found in the things of the world: success, education, career, money, religion, revenge, hatred—but it *can* be found. Christ, the Prince of Peace, is the only means to our wholeness with God and others: *"Peace I leave with you; my peace I give you. I do not give to you as the world gives"* (John 14:27).

The gift of true peace is a blessing given to those raised in Him; it's an assurance offered by the hand of the King. It is a mercy only He can give. This peace begins with our covenant relationship with Him. It flourishes, both inside and out, as we surrender our hearts and lives to His purpose. *"The fruit of that righteousness will be peace; its effect ... will be quietness and confidence forever"* (Isaiah 32:17).

LET PEACE RULE

Paul's exhortation to experience peace doesn't stop there. It further entreats us to let peace *rule* in our hearts. This is another telling word in the original language. In the Greek, the word for *rule* is *brabeuo*[4], meaning to *arbitrate, act as umpire—to make the call in a conflict between contending forces.*

This means that when there is a question, peace acts as an umpire and makes the call on how to respond. It is the reigning standard for deciding what the appropriate action is for healing.

When peace rules in our hearts, we are always looking to mend what is broken; to find restoration and reconciliation. When peace rules in our hearts, our desire is the quietness and rest where sacred wholeness exists.

MAKE EVERY EFFORT

"Let us therefore make every effort to do what leads to peace" (Romans 14:19).

All relationships, no matter how intimate, are bound to encounter conflict and, sadly, feelings are bound to be hurt. Communicating our hurts is not always easy, and resolving the breakdown of our relationships because of those hurts can sometimes feel monumental. When a once-intimate relationship suffers enough conflict, it is a natural response for one or both involved to withdraw their heart from the other. Tending to the conflicts in their early stages is essential in the prevention of this withdrawal and the inevitable loss of relationship.

Driven by the idea of being peacemakers, it may seem that the heart of peace should push offenses or issues aside or that it would simply ignore the feelings that accompany those issues. Small or insignificant irritations should, without a doubt, be handled this way—hearts driven by love do not offend easily. However, when significant hurts are felt, frustrations mount, grudges are harbored, and relationship begins to break down, something must be done to repair it.

The true nature of peacemaking is about doing what is necessary to mend what is broken. To "make every effort" means to pursue or eagerly chase something. God wants peace for us so that we may be whole and restored. We must be diligent and eager to pursue that healing; doing our best, *"as far as it depends on you, live at peace with everyone"* (Romans 12:18).

I am not an expert on the subject of conflict resolution. I wish I were. I wish that I could say that every conflict that I've tried to resolve has turned out exactly the way I wanted it to—or the way God wanted it to. Unfortunately, it hasn't.

Even so, the God-principles of restoring relationship remain. The Father has given a number of clear directives in His Word for resolving disagreements between His people. Done His way, it can yield holy and peace-filled results.

A fundamental part of resolving conflict in any relationship must start with both parties agreeing on an all-important truth: the relationship is valued enough to do whatever it takes to mend the brokenness that has occurred.

For true godly healing to take place, the desire to lovingly and respectfully gain what was lost must be held at the forefront at all times. Restoration and reconciliation take a mutual and intentional decision: an exerted effort to let peace, not anger, rule the situation.

How do we let peace *rule* in conflict?

- *Go and tell them*—not others (Matthew 18:15).
- *Invite the Holy Spirit* into the conversation through prayer and surrender before you begin sharing (Romans 8:26).
- *Assume the positive.* Assume that intentions are pure, even though feelings may be hurt, hearts may be tender, or frustrations may have mounted (Philippians 4:8). [When meeting together, consider trying this: Lay both of your hands palms up, one on each of your knees, as you share with each other. This posture creates an open-hearted stance and prevents angry gestures such as clenching of fists, flailing arms, pointing fingers, etc.].
- *Pour love and grace* on each other. Realizing that God's grace is abundant in the midst of our imperfections, be willing to pour grace on each other and their imperfections (John 1:16).
- Covered in the grace garment of humility, *be willing to hear,* as well as to share. Valuing and honoring each other,

even in the most difficult moments, means being open to receive words of challenge as much as you are willing to share them (James 1:19, 20).

When sharing your hurts with others:

- *Remain calm and kind.*
- Share how you *feel* as a result of the actions of the other.
- Resist judging motives, hearts, or making accusations of *why* you think the actions occurred (i.e. "you did that because...").
- *Stay focused* on the issue at hand, not being tempted to bring up old wounds and offenses that are irrelevant to the resolution of this issue.
- *Share Needs/Wants.* What needs do you have that aren't being met in this situation? What do you need from the person with whom you are sharing? What do you want from that person so that you can move forward?
- *Be willing to hear the response* of the one with whom you've shared and ready to accept a new perspective of the situation, if needed. Consider the possibility that there may be reasons beyond your understanding that may have caused the hurtful actions, and be ready to accept a new way of seeing things that will help you move forward.

- *Ask for/offer forgiveness.* Leave the conversation with a willingness to forgive each other, put the matter to rest, and to move forward in love and a deeper awareness.

When hearing the hurts of others:

- *Remain calm and kind.*
- *Be a good listener* without interrupting the one sharing.
- *Receive the shared feelings* without judging whether right or wrong.
- Be willing to *give a loving response* to the things shared. Ask good questions, repeat what you believe you heard, clarify meaning of what is shared, then lovingly respond or explain your perspective on the situation, if needed.
- *Take ownership* of the necessary areas of your behavior. Be open and willing to adjust or change whatever actions you have been made aware of that are/may have been hurtful, offering what is needed to heal the hearts of others and to restore your relationship.
- *Ask for/Offer Forgiveness.* Leave the conversation with a willingness to forgive one another, put the matter to rest, and to move forward in love and a deeper awareness.

Satan is a trouble-maker and a liar. He wants our God-given relationships to fail miserably; to break down the body of Christ so it can't support itself. Sometimes he tries to convince us that our differences are best handled by venting our frustrations to others, talking about someone behind their back, sending out letters to complain about them, or simply refusing to speak to them anymore. This, faithful one, is not the truth. This is not the behavior of hearts set on Christ.

When we handle conflict in this way, our garments of grace become muddy, and the glory of the King cannot be seen in them. Instead, He calls us to diligently pursue the peace that is offered by His hand, for His people; healed, whole, complete, where we are supposed to be.

"The LORD bless you and keep you; the LORD make his face shine on you and be gracious to you; the LORD turn his face toward you and give you peace" (Numbers 6:24-26).

UR WORLD OF CONFLICT, which is empty, mixed up, and hurting, looks for peace and filling in things that have no value in the heavenly places. Jesus said He came to give us peace, but not the peace as the world gives (John 14:27)—the peace that God gives. The true peace of God seeks not to fix a broken and transient world, but to mend the shattered relationships between Him and His people; to join together that which has been torn apart.

We were created by a loving God to share a loving relationship with Him, to have a deep fellowship with the Creator and King. Yet, our wayward hearts often hinder that. Our sins sever our precious communion with Him (Isaiah 59:2) and we are left broken, empty, and longing.

True peace, the mending of what is broken, can only come from one source—the Prince of Peace, Jesus Christ. *"Love and faithfulness meet together; righteousness and peace kiss each other"* (Psalm 85:10). There is no separating His mercy from His truth, just as there is no separating righteousness from peace. They go hand-in-hand. *"The fruit of that righteousness will be peace; its effect will be quietness and confidence forever"* (Isaiah 32:17).

REFLECTION

1. Close your eyes and picture *peace* in your mind's eye. Write here what you imagined.

2. In Colossians 3:15, Paul said to *"let the peace of Christ rule in your hearts."* Define the peace to which he was referring in this context.

3. To what places do we sometimes look for wholeness? Do you struggle to find wholeness in these places? If so, which ones?

4. Where can you find the gift of *true peace*?

5. What did Paul mean when he said to let peace *rule* in your hearts?

6. While making every effort to do what leads to peace, what is a fundamental part of resolving conflict?

7. What are the five elements of *letting peace rule* in conflict?

8. When in conflict, which of these elements do you do well?

9. In which of these areas do you need to improve? How do you think it will change the outcome?

Nothing More Precious
Chapter 7

"There is nothing more precious than a grateful child
—the opposite is also true."

*T*HIS IS ONE OF the isms we adopted in our home as we raised our six children. I came to realize over the course of our childrearing and our ministry how important the idea of gratefulness was and continues to be. Ungratefulness can play a major role in unpleasant attitudes: rebellion, pride, bitterness, anger, unrealistic expectations, selfishness, and so many more.

Even though I know that my motive for serving others should not be to receive thanks, I still like to be appreciated, and I like being with those who have a thankful heart. Though willing to serve no matter the results, I find I want to do more for those who are thankful. Replete with references to thanks and praise, Scripture makes it clear that God likes to be appreciated, too.

AND BE THANKFUL

The idea of putting on thankfulness is not only a common message in all of Scripture, it is peppered throughout Colossians and Paul's other writings, as well. To the Christ-clothes he calls us to wear, he further exhorts us to, *"Be thankful"* (Colossians 3:15). Our royal wardrobe can't be complete without this all-important article.

In Romans 1, Paul speaks to the foolishness of ungrateful hearts. He paints a bleak picture of the depravity of the people there and warns them of the coming wrath of God because of their sin.

"The wrath of God is being revealed ... since what may be known about God is plain to them, because God has made it plain to them. For since the creation of the world God's invisible qualities—his eternal power and divine nature—have been clearly seen, being understood from what has been made, so that people are without excuse.

For although they knew God, they neither glorified him as God nor gave thanks to him, but their thinking became futile and their foolish hearts were darkened. Although they claimed to be wise, they became fools and exchanged the glory of the immortal God for images made to look like a mortal human being and birds and animals and reptiles" (Romans 1:18-23).

Their sin was two-fold; they neither glorified Him nor gave thanks to Him.

Paul reminds us that the nature of who God is should be obvious just by witnessing the beauty of creation. We have no excuse. We should be able to walk outside and see the clouds, the flowers, the trees; hear the birds, feel the sunshine, the gentle breeze—and *know*. Because evidence of the Creator is all around us, we have a clear glimpse into His divine nature. And in that understanding, we should be thankful.

When there is no thankfulness, Paul says, thinking becomes futile and hearts become dark; leading to depravity of every kind. *"… filled with every kind of wickedness, evil, greed and depravity"* (Romans 1:29).

Being ungrateful isn't just a state of not appreciating or not recognizing. Ungratefulness leads to sin.

THANKFUL IN PRAISE

Jesus was on His way to Jerusalem and traveling a road near the border of Samaria and Galilee, when ten men met Him along the way. Covered with leprosy, deemed unclean, and required by law to keep their distance, they shouted from across the road and begged, *"Jesus, Master, have pity on us"* (Luke 17:11-13).

Leprosy wasn't curable by the modern medicine of that day. These men, stricken with a debilitating disease that destroys flesh and body, knew that the man they saw on the road that day was the only One who could heal them; the only One who could change their future from society's untouchables to ones embraced.

When Jesus saw the men from across the road, He extended His hand of mercy and offered them what they asked for. These broken, hurting men wasted no time in following His instruction to go show themselves to the priests, *"And as they went, they were cleansed"* (Luke 17:14). Can you imagine what their departure looked like?

Beth Moore imagines the scene this way:

"Can you picture them turning their palms up and down with amazement, running to one another, laughing and expressing their joy in stereo? When they clapped their hands with celebration, they felt the welcome sting of healthy flesh. What an exhibition passed through the simple village that day! Who could have missed it? Ten lepers made

whole. Their hair still unkempt and their clothes still torn, but for once they were oblivious. Glad spectacles were they."[1]

But only *one* came back.

Jesus asked, "Were not all ten cleansed? Where are the other nine"? Was no one found to return and give praise to God except this foreigner?" (Luke 17:17,18).

Only one of the ten, when he saw he was healed, came back praising God. Only one threw himself at the Savior's feet and thanked Him. Only one, given the gift he had begged for, returned to acknowledge the One who had offered it.

The leper came back praising Him and thanking Him because a heart clothed in thankfulness just naturally spills over into praise. The two go hand-in-hand.

"Oh give thanks to the Lord; call upon his name; make known his deeds among the peoples! Sing to him, sing praises to him; tell of all his wondrous works!" (1 Chronicles 16:8-9, ESV).

God wants to be recognized for what He has done. He wants us to acknowledge the wondrous works of His hands and the blessings of His enduring love; to openly express our thankfulness and make it known.

THANKFUL IN REMEMBERING

Enslaved, oppressed, and mistreated by the Egyptians, the Israelites begged God for deliverance. Hearing their desperate cry, He orchestrated an awesome rescue plan. With Moses and Aaron as His mouthpiece, He called the Pharaoh to let His people go. When Pharaoh refused, God sent miraculous signs and *incentives* in the form of plagues to convince him. But it did not move him.

With the Pharaoh still unwilling to free His people, God dealt a devastating blow; one that would take the firstborn son of every Egyptian household. After warning the Israelites and instructing them to paint their doorways with lamb's blood so the destroyer would pass over their home, the Lord struck down the firstborn of every creature. There was anguish and wailing throughout Egypt. With this, Pharaoh finally gave in and drove the Israelites away.

Gathering God's people (possibly three million pilgrims), Moses led them out of the country. Scripture tells us that *"the Lord kept vigil that night to bring them out of Egypt"* (Exodus 12:42) and that

He also gave them a directive on how to *remember* what He'd done for them that night. This remembering would later come to be known as *The Passover*.

As they marched out of Egypt, Pharaoh's hardened heart reconsidered his decision. The Egyptian troops set out in hot pursuit of the Israelites. But the angel of the Lord went before them and protected them. He directed Moses to raise his staff to part the sea so His people could walk through the wall of water, then again lower it to swallow up the Egyptians as they entered in. We are told that when the Israelites *"saw the great power of the Lord displayed ... they put their trust in him"* (Exodus 14:31).

Unfortunately, their trust didn't last. Before long they were complaining about their drinking water, their food, their conditions; complaining to Moses and grumbling against the Lord over and over. Again and again the Lord would provide for them, protect them, care for them—again and again they would forget. Their continued grumbling caused God's anger to burn against them. He sent snakes—and fire. He threatened to destroy them. Thankfully, Moses talked Him out of that. Eventually, He withheld their blessings. They missed out on what He wanted to give them—a land of milk and honey. They missed out because they failed to see what God had done, and they didn't remember *to be thankful.*

Reading over the story of how God took the Israelites from slavery to freedom and how they seemed to be oblivious to His constant care made me laugh a little. Seriously? How could they not see it? I guess it would be funny—*if*. It would be easy to judge them *if* we weren't just the same.

We so often spend our time dwelling on the things that are wrong with our lives—or other people. We mumble and grumble about all the problems in the church; how one person did or didn't do what we wanted them to do. We focus on what we don't have, instead of what we do have. We see the ugly instead of the beautiful; becoming negative and hard to be with. We can make the people around us feel exhausted with our demanding and grumpy attitudes. We can miss out on what God wants to give us—riches untold; all because we fail to see His hand at work, and we don't remember to be thankful.

COUNT YOUR MANY BLESSINGS

The Bible is filled with God's directives on remembering: the Passover feast, the jar of manna, the festivals, the Ark of the Covenant, the Lord's Supper.

God told the Israelites to keep the memories of what He had done for generations to come; to recall them in their own hearts, to remember together. So that we can recall what He's done in our lives, He wants us to keep our memories, too.

I had a little spiral "gratefulness journal" where I had been keeping a list of my blessings: grandbaby giggles, hot water, teacups, email, friendship, sunsets, hot chocolate chip cookies, and more. I saw it lying on my desk as I was packing my bags to go home—to go home to bury my son. I know it must have been the Holy Spirit that prompted me to grab it and throw it in my suitcase because I don't think it would have crossed my mind otherwise.

Over the next few weeks, I continued to list the blessings that He was giving me even in the darkest moments of my life. It wasn't until many months later that I realized what a great gift that practice would turn out to be. You see, my mind had been so muddled in the midst of my grief, I hadn't remembered much of what I'd written.

Reading later over each blessing, both big and little, reminded me that I had never been alone; each one discrediting Satan's whispers that if God's love was real, He would have saved my son. Like everyone who has suffered deep loss, I've journeyed through some hard places in my grief. There have been times when the pain was so raw and the days were so dark, I was sure

I'd fall off the precipice I imagined myself standing on. But that notebook and its list that I later came to call "The Shapes and Sizes of God's Comfort," saved me from despair on my most sorrowful days; the days when I needed to remember how He had provided for me, protected me, and cared for me. Remembering was my hope—and my joy.

Clothing ourselves in the grace of thankfulness is an intentional choice to take notice of what God has done for us; remembering the faithfulness of the King and praising Him for the many blessings He offers. Maybe you'd like to do what I have. If so, grab yourself a little notebook and write down five things each day that you are thankful for—just five things—each day. Then, pick it up often and read it over and over again. Tomorrow. Next week. Next year. Keep writing. Keep reading.

Keep the memories so that you can recall what He has done; so that the shapes and sizes of His comfort and provision are evident to you. I have no doubt that God will use the smallest of your recorded blessings to reassure you of His presence and His care. Your heart will be wrapped in the garments of gratitude. Your contentment will be overflowing. Your joy will be unending.

$\mathcal{U}$SING THE LUNCH of a small boy to feed the multitudes, Jesus looked up into heaven and gave thanks. He stood before a tomb where his friend lay dead, called him forth, and gave thanks. Sitting around a table in the upper room with His disciples, knowing His heart would soon know betrayal, knowing His body would soon know suffering, knowing His Father would soon turn His face away—Jesus gave thanks.

Praising God with thankfulness for the blessings in our lives, not only brings Glory to the Father but gives us a new perspective; a negative attitude replaced by a positive one. Recognizing that all good and perfect gifts come from Him instills humility, breeds contentment, and envelops us in peaceful joy.

Paul reminds, *"Rejoice always, pray continually, give thanks in all circumstances"* (1 Thessalonians 5:16-18). Though we often forget, thanking the Father for the good gifts He gives, is not all that hard to understand.

But—in ALL circumstances?

How do we give thanks for the hard things; for tragedy, for grief and loss, for financial troubles, for failing health? God has not asked us to see bad things as good. He has asked us to see that *He* is good even in the midst of them; knowing *"that in all things God works for the good of those who love him"* (Romans 8:28).

Like Jesus, with the knowledge and trust of God's promised blessings even out of the most difficult of circumstances, our gratitude overflows into an unending joy that reflects the glory of the King.

REFLECTION

1. What unpleasant attitudes can be the result of ungratefulness?

2. Read Romans 1:18-23. What does Paul say happens to those with ungrateful hearts?

3. In Luke 17, we read how Jesus healed ten lepers. When He was telling the story, He made a point to mention that only one came back to thank Him. What was significant about the one who came back?

4. Write out 1 Chronicles 16:8-9 here. Underline each directive meant to show gratefulness to God for His blessings.

5. God blessed the Israelites over and over, yet their forgetfulness caused them to lose trust. Recall the areas of blessing in your life. Has your forgetfulness caused you to lose trust in Him?

6. What has God had to do to remind you of His blessings?

7. Are there areas in your life where you tend to complain and grumble? If so, write a prayer asking God to help you overcome your negative perspective.

8. Reminder: "There is nothing more _____ than a _____ _____; the _____ is _____ _____."

Your Meant to Be
Chapter 8

*I*N THE YEARS OF MY MINISTRY and in my role as a Christian Life Coach, I've been honored to journey with many of God's women; coming alongside them and supporting them as they strive to fulfill the purpose to which He has called them. This isn't always easy. The idea of purpose can be a difficult one to grasp when struggling to understand just exactly what He wants us to do for Him.

The truth is, I've spent a lot of my life trying to grasp that understanding, too. *Why am I here, Lord? What are your plans for me? What do you want me to do for you, Lord? What is my mission? What is my purpose? What is my meant-to-be?*

What He began to whisper back to me was not what I expected.

IN PURSUIT OF PURPOSE

My journey to fully understanding my *meant-to-be* happened in a country not my own; a place where I expected to have a clear purpose. I fully intended to be well-used and used up; certain I'd be fulfilled doing the work I had been gifted to do.

I had given several years to raising my six children: homeschooling them, training them, nurturing them, showing them the world—then giving them wings. My nest was suddenly empty, and I then had freedom to serve alongside my husband on the mission field again. I had looked forward to our mission work with excitement and anticipation as we made our way around the world together, just the two of us, to realize our shared vision. But our mission work didn't turn out the way we thought it would. Our mission looked more like *his* mission, *his* work—and I was left wondering what *my* place should be; what *I* should do to be about the Lord's work there.

I had read all those "bloom where you are planted" lessons. I had taught them many times myself. But I wasn't feeling like I was blooming. I felt more like I was withering. I felt like my energy was slowly being drained from me; unused, unneeded, and unappreciated. Though surrounded by kind and loving people, I had never felt more alone. I begged God to show me

116

the work He had for me to do in this place. I begged Him for my purpose to become obvious; for the reason He had asked me to leave my treasured ones on the other side of the world. I continued to cry out, *What do You want me to do for You, Lord? Please show me what You want me to do for You.*

In response to my steady plea He began quietly speaking to my heart. Not volumes. Not epistles. Just one word. One message. *"Be."*

I remember, as a young Christian, the first time I heard a sermon based on Psalm 37:4, *"Take delight in the LORD, and he will give you the desires of your heart."* I'm not sure if it was something the preacher said or just what I mistakenly understood, but I left believing that the focus of this verse was the promise to give me what I deeply wanted. I bowed before the Lord and fervently prayed for the pressing desire of my heart at that time—to find the father who'd left me as a small child. As evidence of God's patient love, He gave me exactly what I asked for, even though He knew that what I asked for would not fill the longing of my heart. It would be a while before I knew it, too. It would take a lot of heartache and more rejection from my earthly father to help me realize that the Father I truly longed for was the One who had been by my side all along.

God has given us a heart that desires, longs, and hopes for fulfillment in Him but, as in those early years, once again I was looking for my filling in the wrong places and from the wrong things. Timothy Keller says, *"Our need for worth is so powerful that whatever we base our identity and value on, we essentially 'deify.'"* I hadn't realized it, but in many ways, my craving for worth and significance, even in my service to the Lord, had become my idol. My pursuit of what I understood as purpose had unwittingly become more important than my pursuit of the One who gives it.

"Be"

When Paul told the Colossian brethren to *"let the word of Christ dwell in you richly"* (Colossians 3:16, ESV), I believe his message was the same. He had told them to set their minds on Christ and to cover themselves with who He was. Now he was telling them to let Christ live in their hearts; for Him to be comfortable and *at home in them*[1]—in us. Paul's words, like those of the psalmist who said, *"... you will fill me with joy in your presence"* (Psalm 16:11), were a reminder to take delight in the company of the Lord.

"Be"

A TEACHER OF THE LAW asked Jesus what the most important commandment was. He answered, *" 'Love the Lord your God with all your heart and with all your soul and with all your mind and with all your strength'. The second is this: 'Love your neighbor as yourself.' There is no commandment greater than these"* (Mark 12:30-31).

The "greatest command" embodies all that God wants for us: to live in His presence, to have a personal and intimate love-relationship with Him, and to radiate His glory in such a way that our lives draw others to Himself. God's *ultimate purpose* for us, our meant-to-be, isn't about what we do; it's about where our hearts dwell.

"Be"

Be *still* in Him. Be *with* Him. Be *filled* in Him. Be *fulfilled* in Him.

EVERYDAY LIFE: ON MISSION LIVING

Our life is a journey that has many paths and stops along the way. Our seasons change. Our circumstances change. Our skills and abilities change. The job, *the mission*, that He calls us to *do* at any given time, changes. Each mission becomes the outgrowth of our being—first the *being*, then the *doing*.

Paul wraps up the part of his letter that calls for our spiritual makeover with this admonition, *"And whatever you do, whether in word or deed, do it all in the name of the Lord Jesus, giving thanks to God the Father through him"* (Colossians 3:17).

This is the essence of a life on purpose—of life *on mission*.

Life on mission isn't just a one-time thing. It's a daily walk with God; first building that deep and intimate relationship with Him, stepping where He steps, then making a mark on the lives and hearts of those around us. It is for every season and every stage of our journey; every circumstance and anywhere we may make our home at the time—growing, flourishing, and blooming exactly where we are planted.

Living on mission is an intentional choice to give over to His plan for His purpose—doing whatever we do, no matter what it is, in the name of the King and for His glory.

BECAUSE YOU SAY SO, I WILL

They had worked all night with nothing to show for it. They were calling it quits and washing their nets when Jesus noticed their boats at the water's edge. People were crowding around him to hear the Word of God, so He stepped into the boat that belonged to Peter and asked him to push away from the shore. When Jesus finished teaching the people, He told Peter to go into deeper water so they could catch some fish (Luke 5:1-4).

I often wonder what Peter may have been thinking that morning as he sat in the boat with Jesus. Was he weary, frustrated, or discouraged from all his laboring with no results? Did he feel defensive that Jesus would question his ability as a fisherman? That He would suggest that he let down his nets to fish, as if they hadn't already been doing that for the entire night?

I'm not exactly sure what he was feeling; I can only speculate. What I can be sure of, because Scripture tells us, is that he objected a little, *"Master, we've worked hard all night and haven't caught anything"* (vs. 5).

He may have questioned Jesus in the moment but even in his doubt, his heart softened as quickly as it had reacted. And—he surrendered. *"But because you say so, I will"* (Luke 5:5). Even though he may not have understood the reasoning behind Jesus' directive, Peter surrendered and obeyed.

It was to this yielded heart that Jesus began to pour the blessing of fish so abundant that Peter's nets and his boat couldn't contain them. So many fish that the nets and the boats of his friends couldn't contain them. And Scripture says they were astonished. Peter, knowing he was in the presence of the Holy One, fell at His knees. I imagine Jesus reaching down with His tender touch to reassure him and with a hint of what was ahead, He said to Simon, *"Don't be afraid; from now on you will fish for people"* (Luke 5:10). Peter and his friends would no longer be doing fish-fishing; they would be doing Kingdom-fishing—rescuing the hearts of men.

Peter's initial response to Jesus' request is so—*me*. The truth is, I can often be opinionated about how I should serve God; what *I* would like to do for Him, what *I* think my mission should be or how *I* should accomplish the task He's given me. Like Peter, I sometimes question Him in the moment, thinking I have a good plan for the path I should take. My ideas, however awesome they may be, aren't always the ones the Lord has in mind, and He's quick to remind me that it's okay to plan my future as long as I remember Who is in control of it: *"In their hearts humans plan their course, but the Lord establishes their steps"* (Proverbs 16:9).

Scripture tells us that Peter and his friends left everything to begin walking on mission with Jesus. If I'm to walk on mission with Him, I must also be yielding and moldable like Peter was, allowing the Lord to decide where I'm going and what I'm going to do, even when it's not the way I had envisioned it or when it may not make sense to my feeble understanding.

It wasn't until Peter surrendered his heart and obeyed, that Jesus would offer him His full blessing, a blessing so abundant it couldn't be contained. It wasn't until Peter's heart was softened to the will of his Master, that Jesus would call him to something more—something Kingdom-sized.

It's when our hearts are set on things above and surrendered to His direction, that He can astonish us with the outpouring of His blessings. It's when our heart softens to the will of the King, that He moves us from earthly ambitions to Kingdom purpose. That's where our fulfillment lies.

We are God's women on mission. Meant-to-*BE*. Sitting at the table of the King; feasting and receiving our filling there. Surrounded by the glory of His presence. Fulfilled by Him and Him alone.

This is our purpose. This is *your* purpose.

This is your *meant-to-be*!

OUR SPIRITUAL MAKEOVER is in progress. Our transformation journey has just begun. We've rid ourselves of the old and tattered clothes from the life we used to live, and we stand before the closet of the King.

I pray that in our short time together, you've become confident in the knowledge of your true identity. You are a daughter of the King, and He desires a deep and intimate relationship with you. He cherishes you. He adores you. He has redeemed you. You are His—and He wants everyone to know it.

Our garments of His grace are ready; colored, designed, and fitted uniquely for each of us and the gifts He's entrusted into our hands. With each heart-action, we testify to our royal heritage. With each offer of true forgiveness, each decision to pursue godly peace, each thankful "hallelujah," and each demonstration of God-love—His glory shines in and through us; revealing the King's heart to those who have never known Him.

Though the journey ahead may not be an easy one, we are all in this together; walking alongside, cheering one another on, and holding each other up when we get tired. Together, we will strive to hear His direction and surrender to His will. We will be intentional to dwell in His presence. We will seek to live every day on mission; doing whatever we do, no matter what it is, in His name.

"When Christ, who is your life, appears, then you also will appear with him in glory" (Colossians 3:4).

One day we'll all feast together around the King's table. We'll know how to find one another; we'll be the ones—***Divinely Dressed.***

REFLECTION

1. What comes to mind when you hear the word *purpose*? In what ways have you struggled in understanding your purpose?

2. Read Paul's words in Colossians 3:16 (ESV). How do you think they relate to God's ultimate purpose, His *meant-to-be*, for you?

3. What *"Be"* message may God be speaking to you today?

4. What does it mean to live a life *on mission*?

5. In what ways have you walked on mission in your Christ-life?

6. Peter made a choice to surrender to Jesus, even when he didn't fully understand the logic in His directive. To what areas of your life has God called you to surrender, even when it didn't seem logical?

7. How did God astonish you with blessings when you yielded and allowed Him to be in control?

8. In what areas are you still struggling to surrender and obey? How will you work toward yielding in these areas?

9. What kingdom-sized mission do you think God is calling your softened heart to embrace?

ℋotes

Chapter 1 - Identification Review

1. "Struggle", Strong's Concordance, *agon*, 73

Chapter 2 - Out with the Old

1. "Put to Death", Strong's Concordance, *nekros*, 3498
2. *Colossians & Philemon*, Bob Martin
3. "Unwholesome", Strong's Concordance, 4550

Chapter 3 - Putting on Garments of Grace

1. "Clothed", Strong's Concordance 17469, 1463
2. The Journey of a Grieving Heart [Blog by Penny J. Kendall].
thejourneyofagrievingheart.com
3. *On Death & Dying* by Elisabeth Kübler-Ross 1969
4. "Patience", *Theological Dictionary of the New Testament*, Vol 4,
pp.374-375

Chapter 4 - The Prisoner's Key

1. "Forgiveness", Strong's Concordance, 5483
2. "Forbearance", Strong's Concordance, *anechomai*, G430
3. *Life-Changing Love*—John Ortberg

Chapter 5 - The Crimson Thread

1. "Love", Strong's Concordance, *agape*, 25
2. "Honor", Strong's Concordance, 5091
2. *Love Does: Discover a Secretly Incredible Life in an Ordinary World*—Bob Goff

Chapter 6 - Binding the Broken

1. "Peace", Strong's Concordance, *eirene*, 1515
2. *What They Did Yesterday Afternoon*—Poem by Warsan Shire

Chapter 7 - Nothing More Precious

1. *Jesus, The One and Only*—Beth Moore

Chapter 8 - Becoming Your Meant-to-Be

1. "Dwell", Strong's Concordance *enoikeo*, 1774

Bibliography

Goff, Bob (2012*), Love Does: Discover A Secretly Incredible Life in an Ordinary World*. Nashville, TN: Thomas Nelson.

Kubler-Ross M.D., Elisabeth (1969), *On Death & Dying*. New York, NY: Scribner.

Lewis, C.S (1952, 1980), *Mere Christianity*. New York, NY: Harper One.

Holy Bible, New International Version, Copyright 1973, 1978, 1984, 2011 by Biblica, Inc.

Hold Bible, New Living Translation, Copyright 1996, 2004, 2007 by Tyndale House Publishers, Inc.

Horst, J. (1964—), G Kittel, G.W. Bromiley, & G. Friedrich (Eds.), *Theological dictionary of the New Testament* (electronic ed., Vol 4, p. 375). Grand Rapids, MI: Eerdmans.

Keller, Timothy (2008), *The Reason for God*, New York, NY: Dutton-Penguin Group.

Ortberg, John (1998), *Love Beyond Reason: Moving God's Love from Your Head to Your Heart*. Grand Rapids, MI: Zondervan.

Martin, Bob (1999). *Colossians and Philemon: Introductory New Testament Studies*. Lubbock, Tx: Sunset International Bible Institute.

Moore, Beth (2013), *Jesus, the One and Only*. Nashville, TN: B&H Publishing Group.

Nouwen, Henri, McNeill, Donald P. and Morrison, Douglas A. (1982), *Compassion: A Reflection on the Christian Life*. New York, NY: Double Day.

Smede, Lewis (2007), *Forgive and Forget: Healing the Hurts We Don't Deserve*. New York, NY: Harper One.

Shire, Warsan (2011), *Teaching My Mother How to Give Birth*. United Kingdom: Flipped Eye Publishing.

Strong, J. (1996), *The exhaustive concordance of the Bible; Showing every word of text of the common English version of the canonical books, and ever occurrence of each word in regular order*. Electronic edition. Ontario: Woodside Bible Fellowship.

 For Additional Copies or
Info on Qty Discounts
Please Contact Us At
hello@pennyjkendall.com